The Young Geographer Investigates

Rivers

Terry Jennings

Oxford University Press

Oxford University Press, Walton Street, Oxford OX2 6DP

Oxford   New York   Toronto
Delhi   Bombay   Calcutta   Madras   Karachi
Kuala Lumpur   Singapore   Hong Kong   Tokyo
Nairobi   Dar es Salaam   Cape Town
Melbourne   Auckland   Madrid

and associated companies in
Berlin   Ibadan

Oxford is a trade mark of Oxford University Press

ISBN 0 19 917073 8 (Paperback)
First published 1986
Reprinted 1988, 1990, 1991, 1993

ISBN 0 19 917079 7 (Hardback)
First published 1986
Reprinted 1988, 1990, 1991, 1993

© Terry Jennings

Typeset in Great Britain by
Tradespools Ltd., Frome, Somerset
Printed in Hong Kong

Acknowledgements

The publishers would like to thank the following for permission to reproduce transparencies:

Heather Angel p. 40; ANPFoto p. 29 (bottom right), p. 30; Derek Fordham/
Arctic Camera p. 4 (centre right); Aspect Picture Library p. 12 (bottom), p. 26
(top right and cover), p. 31 (centre right), p. 34 (centre right), p. 35 (top right),
p.36 (bottom right), p. 38 (bottom left); Camerapix Hutchison Library p. 32
(centre); Bruce Coleman/Zuber p. 4 (bottom right), Coleman/Crichton p. 6 (top
right), Coleman/Kage p. 7 (centre right), Coleman/Molyneux p. 13 (centre
right), Coleman/Harris p. 17 (top left), Coleman/Reinhard p. 27 (bottom right),
Coleman/Thompson p. 28 (top right), Coleman/Burton p. 28 (bottom right),
Coleman/Goulston p. 36 (bottom left), Coleman/Krasemann p. 15 (bottom left),
Coleman/Leonard Lee Rue III p. 37 (right), Coleman/Shaw p. 42; Robert
Estall p. 31 (top right); Tim Furniss p. 13 (bottom left); Ray Green p. 38 (top);
Sally & Richard Greenhill p. 33 (bottom left, bottom right), p. 35 (centre left),
p. 38 (centre right); Susan Griggs/Photofile p. 10 (top), Griggs/Yeomans p. 31
(bottom left), Griggs/St. Maur Sheil p. 31 (bottom right), Griggs/O'Rear p. 46
(bottom left); Robert Harding/Sassoon p. 6 (centre right), Harding/Waltham
p. 14 (bottom right), Robert Harding p. 17 (inset); Eric Hosking p. 27 (centre),
Alan Hutchison/Von Puttkamer p. 32 (centre left), Hutchison/House p. 32
(bottom right), Hutchison/Taylor p. 34 (bottom right), Hutchison/Giudicelli
p. 35 (centre right); Terry Jennings p. 4 (left), p. 9 (inset), p. 12 (inset), p. 14
(centre right), p. 16 (centre right), p. 17 (right), p. 18 (centre right), p. 25
(bottom right), p. 26 (centre right, bottom left and right), p. 27 (bottom left,
centre right) p. 29 (top right) p. 40, p. 45; Frank Lane/Chani p. 43; Tony
Morrison p. 8 (top); OSF/Survival Anglia/Campbell p. 11, OSF/Bailey p. 15
(bottom right); Perrard/Rapho p. 18 (bottom right); Shostal Associates p. 37
(left); Spectrum Colour Library p. 5 (bottom right); John Topham Picture
Library p. 18 (top right); West Air Photography p. 13 (top right); Zefa/Kalt
p. 17 (centre left), Zefa/Pfaff p. 29 (centre right)

Illustrated by Stephen Cocking Gary Hincks Peter Joyce Ed McLachlan
Ben Manchipp Tudor Artists

Contents

Water

Most of the Earth is covered by water. Nearly three-quarters of the surface of the Earth is covered by oceans and seas. This water is salty.

There is also a great deal of water on the land. There is water in ponds, lakes, rivers and streams. There is water in ice, particularly in the great ice sheets that cover the Arctic and Antarctic. But on land most of the water is out of sight. It is hidden away in the soil and rocks of the Earth's crust. This water is called ground water. There is also a lot of water in the bodies of living things, including humans. Without water everything would die.

This book is about rivers. Usually these huge ribbons of water flow across the land. A few flow underground. Rivers change the landscape by wearing away the soil and rocks. They carry the pieces down towards the sea, where new land may be formed.

Waves slowly wear away a rocky coastline

An ice sheet in the Arctic

The meandering River Omo in Ethiopia

Rivers and towns and villages

London in Roman times

Many early towns and villages were built near rivers. The rivers stopped enemies from attacking from one side. Water from the rivers could be used by people and animals for drinking. It could also be used to make crops grow. The soil by rivers is often fertile so that crops grow well. Fish in the rivers could be used for food.

Many people used rivers to travel along because the roads were poor. Nowadays roads and railways often follow river valleys where the ground is less steep.

Today many of the world's greatest cities are built close to rivers. Often these cities grew where the river was shallow and could be crossed on foot. Such places are called fords. Many towns and cities are named after these fords. Other towns and cities grew up where the first bridges were built. And large ports grew up at the mouths of rivers where sheltered harbours could be built for ships.

Rivers often also form the boundaries between different countries. The River Rhine in Europe forms a boundary between several different countries.

The Rhine marks the border between France and Germany at Strasbourg

Using water

We humans drink water and use it in many other ways. We use water for cooking and washing up. Water is also used for cleaning clothes, cars, walls and floors. We use water for pleasure when we swim, sail or water-ski. Ships make voyages over water carrying cargoes and people. In places where there is a plentiful supply of water, each person uses on average between 150 and 500 litres a day.

Factories and power stations also use lots of water. Most of this is collected rainwater or comes from rivers, lakes and wells. Although there is plenty of water in the sea, it is difficult to use because of all the salt in it.

There is a limited amount of water on our planet. We have been using the same water for hundreds and

Power Station and barges at Greenwich

Collecting water at Tamil Nadu, India

thousands of years. We can use the same water over and over again because of something called the water cycle.

How much water is used each day in an average house?

The water cycle

water vapour cools and falls as rain or snow

rain forms streams and rivers and returns to the sea

wind and sun evaporate water into clouds

All over the world water is evaporating. This means that the water is turning into an invisible gas called water vapour. The sun shining and the wind blowing on the sea turns a lot of water into water vapour all the time. The water vapour rises into the air. High in the sky it is cold, and the water vapour cools to form clouds.

The tiny drops of water which make a cloud are so small and light that they float in the air. If they are cooled still more, as happens when the clouds rise over a mountain, then the tiny drops of water join together and fall to the ground as rain. When the weather is very cold, the tiny drops of water in the clouds may turn to ice. Each little piece of ice forms a shape called a crystal. The ice crystals grow bigger and bigger and fall as snowflakes.

A magnified snow flake

Some of the rain or melted snow goes into streams or rivers. Streams and rivers always flow downwards. They take the easiest way and carry their water down to the sea. So we are using the same water over and over again. This is what is meant by the water cycle. Rivers are a vital part of this water cycle.

The sources of rivers

Much of the rain which falls on land soaks through the soil. Because soil lets water through, it is said to be permeable. Something which will not let water pass through it is impermeable. If the water cannot pass through the rock layers below the surface, it collects in hollows. There it forms ponds and lakes.

Mostly, though, the rocks are permeable and the water sinks underground. Eventually it may reach impermeable rock. When the water reaches impermeable rock it cannot sink any further. The water runs along the top of the impermeable rock until it finds a way out. In places the water may seep out of the ground as a spring. The water from the spring will form a stream.

The place where a river or stream

A spring near the Dead Sea, said to be where Moses struck the rock

begins is called its source. Many rivers and streams have springs on hills or mountains as their sources. Some rivers have a lake as their source. The River Nile has as its source Lake Victoria. Other rivers flow from the ends of melting glaciers. You can read more about glaciers on page 15.

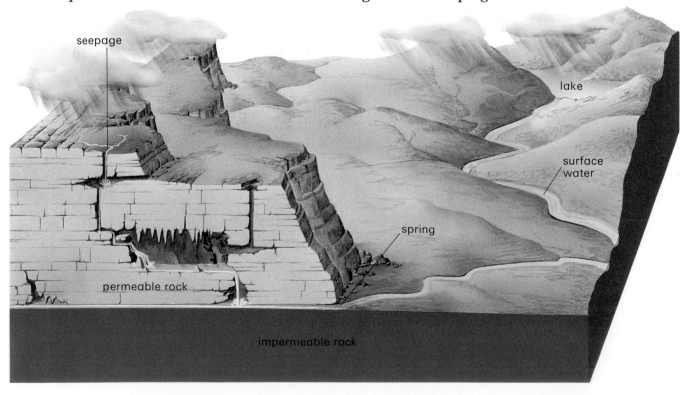

seepage

lake

surface water

spring

permeable rock

impermeable rock

The life of a river

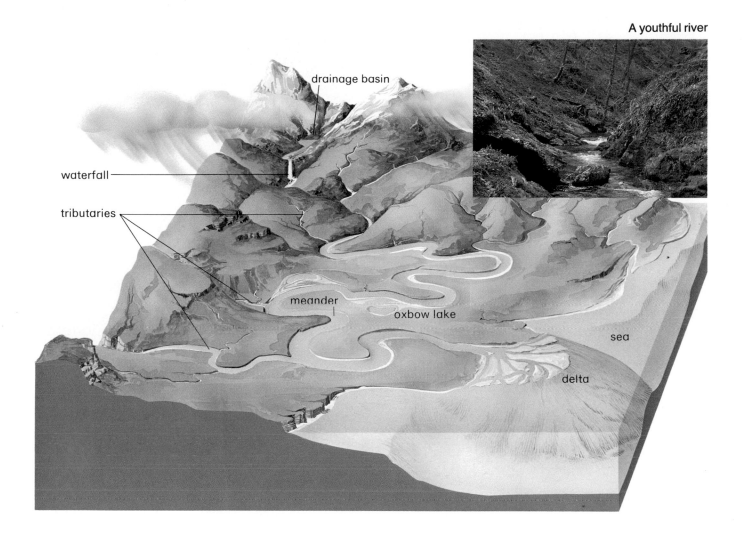

A youthful river

drainage basin

waterfall

tributaries

meander

oxbow lake

sea

delta

The water in a stream flows downhill. Later, other streams join it. The streams which join the main one are called tributaries. When several streams join up they may form a river. There is no real difference between a river and a stream. A river is usually bigger than a stream.

As the river flows downwards it grows as more and more rivers and streams join it. The area of land which supplies a river with water is called its drainage basin. Some large rivers have a drainage basin covering several thousand square kilometres.

A river goes through stages in its life. In its youthful stage a river is flowing fast. Pieces of rock are carried with its water. After heavy rain or when the snow on the mountains melts, the river may carry huge boulders. These pieces of rock grind against each other. They gradually break down into pieces of gravel, sand and mud. The pieces of rock also grind against the bottom and sides of the river. Gradually the river becomes wider and deeper. The process by which rivers wear away rocks and carry the pieces towards the sea is called erosion.

9

Waterfalls

Sometimes the land that rivers travel over suddenly changes level. The water tumbles over the edge, and becomes a waterfall. There are lots of waterfalls along a youthful river.

Waterfalls are formed when a river crosses different kinds of rock. Some rocks, like granite, are very hard. Other rocks, such as chalk and clay, are soft. As the river goes along it wears away the rocks over which it flows. The river can wear away soft rock more easily than hard rock. If a river flows over a hard rock and then over a soft one, the soft rock will be worn away more. At first a little step will be made. Gradually, as more of the soft rock is worn away, the step gets bigger. After thousands of years there may be a large waterfall.

Often the water and pieces of rock swirling around at the bottom of the waterfall wear away a hollow. This hollow at the bottom of the waterfall is called a plunge pool. Sometimes there is more than one plunge pool.

The Yosemite Falls, California

The formation of a waterfall

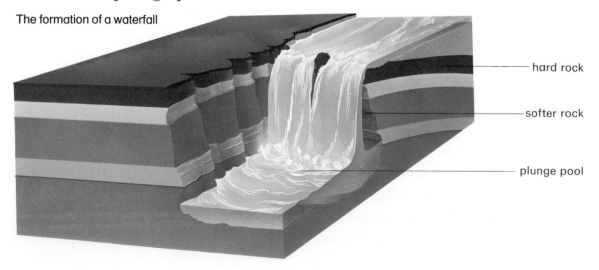

hard rock

softer rock

plunge pool

10

Mature rivers

Eventually the river leaves the hills and mountains behind. It is in its mature stage. Because the ground is less steep, the river flows less quickly. There is more water because more tributaries have joined the river.

Since the water is flowing slowly, it cannot carry boulders and large pieces of rock. But it does carry large quantities of sand, mud and small stones. The river no longer digs down so deeply into its bed. But it still moves fast enough to eat into its banks and to widen its valley. It makes wide S-shaped bends. These are called meanders.

Meanders are formed when the water wears away the outer bank of the river. If a car goes round a sharp bend, the passengers may be thrown to one side. When a river goes round a corner, the water and pieces of rock are thrown to the outside bank. The outside bank is worn away and a small cliff is formed. On the inside of the bend, the water moves more slowly. Here some of the mud, sand and stones sink to the river bed.

A meander in a mature river

Old age

When the river reaches the flat land it winds slowly to the sea. It is now in its old age. In old age the river contains most water. But it is flowing even more slowly and its water is muddy. The river flows so slowly that it carries mostly mud and sand. It no longer erodes the land.

After heavy rain, or when the snow has melted, the river cannot carry away all the water from the hills and mountains. The flat fields nearby are flooded. Any pebbles or larger grains of sand carried by the river are dropped before the water overflows. The stones gradually pile up into high river banks called levees.

Sometimes when it floods, a river changes course. Bends or meanders may be cut off from the main river. These bends form ox-bow lakes which

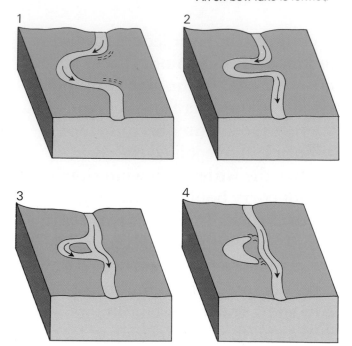

An ox-bow lake is formed

eventually dry up.

When the flood water has gone, the flat fields or 'water meadows' are covered by fine mud. This makes the grass grow well. There is then rich grazing for cattle in the summer.

The shallow bed of a dried up ox-bow lake (centre)

Estuaries or river mouths

A few rivers flow into lakes, but most flow into the sea. When a river flows into the sea we say it has reached its mouth. If the river has a wide mouth this is called an estuary.

The fresh water flowing down the river meets the sea water brought by the tides into the river mouth. The river drops its load of mud and sand. Some of this material is washed away by the sea. Often, though, the mud and sand pile up around the estuary or mouth of the river.

If the tides are not strong where the river enters the sea, the river may split up into several channels. The mud and sand dropped by the river form a delta. This is often shaped like a triangle. The delta is new land. It is made from tiny pieces of rock brought by the river from the hills and mountains.

Above Right: An estuary in south-west England
Right: Dredger on the Dee estuary, North Wales
Below: A satellite's view of the Nile Delta

Some rivers have deep channels where they reach the sea. Ocean-going ships can sail along these. Docks have been built where there is calm, deep water so that the ships can unload their cargoes and passengers in safety. From time to time mud and sand brought by the river may make the channel less deep. Then special ships called dredgers dig away this mud and sand to make the channel deeper again.

Underground rivers

Not all of the rain which falls on mountains and hills goes into streams or rivers. If the hill or mountain is made of limestone, the rainwater quickly soaks into it. This is because limestone is a permeable rock. When rain falls, the water dissolves some of the carbon dioxide gas from the air. This turns the rainwater into a very weak acid. As the rainwater soaks into the limestone it makes cracks in the limestone wider.

Over thousands of years the rainwater may dissolve so much of the limestone that huge caves are formed. If the bottom of the cave is made of a rock which is impermeable, then the water cannot sink any lower. It flows along the bottom of the cave as an underground river or stream.

Often as water drips through the roof of the cave it leaves behind some of the limestone it dissolved. The limestone may slowly form beautiful shapes like icicles. These are called stalactites and stalagmites and they hang from the roof of the cave and grow up from the floor. The stalactites and stalagmites may eventually join up to form pillars.

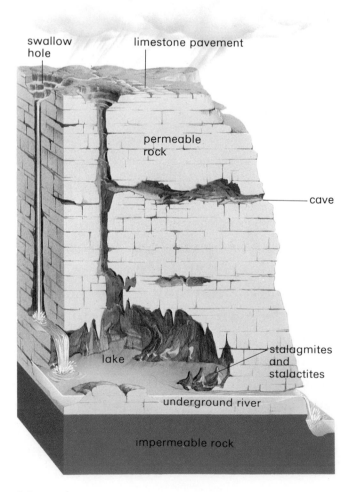

A limestone pavement

Stalactites and stalagmites in Cumbria

14

Glaciers

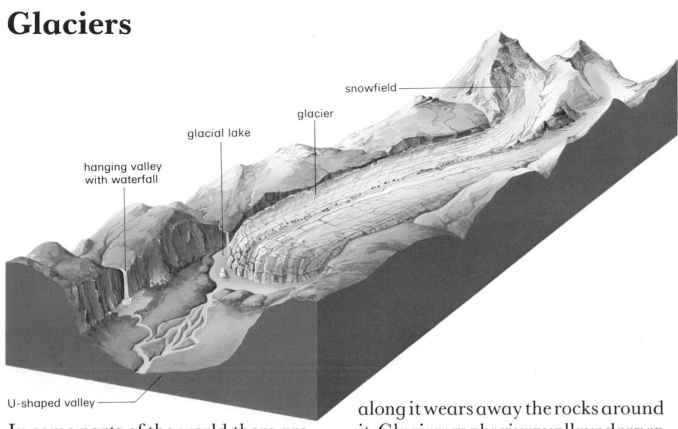

snowfield

glacier

glacial lake

hanging valley with waterfall

U-shaped valley

In some parts of the world there are large rivers of ice. These rivers of ice are called glaciers. Glaciers occur in very cold parts of the world.

When it snows, the snow collects in valleys and hollows. As more and more snow falls, the snow near the ground is crushed into ice by the snow above. All the snow and packed ice slowly slide down the valley. As the glacier creeps

along it wears away the rocks around it. Glaciers make river valleys deeper and U-shaped.

Thousands of years ago the world was much colder than it is today. The world was in what is called the Ice Age. During the Ice Age there were many glaciers. The glaciers made deep U-shaped valleys. We can still see these U-shaped valleys, even where there are no longer any glaciers. Where one glacier flowed over into another it often left what is today called a hanging valley. Many of these valleys now have streams flowing from them as waterfalls.

The edge of a glacier

U-shaped valley with streams

Drinking water

Some of the water we use for drinking comes from wells or springs. But most of our water comes from rivers. The water is kept in big lakes called reservoirs. A large wall, or dam, is built across a river valley. Then a reservoir is formed behind the dam.

From the reservoir the water goes down a pipe to the waterworks. At the waterworks the water is made clean and fit to drink. The water first soaks through beds of sand and gravel. The dirt stays behind in the sand and gravel. Then a gas called chlorine is put into the water to kill any germs. The clean water goes along big pipes under the roads. Other smaller pipes take clean water to the taps in our homes.

Dirty water from our houses goes along a large pipe called a sewer to the sewage works. At the sewage works the dirty water is put into large tanks. Some of the dirt settles out. Then the water passes through layers of sand, gravel or clinker, where all the rest of the dirt gets stuck. The water is now clean enough to go back into a river. It is not clean enough to drink though.

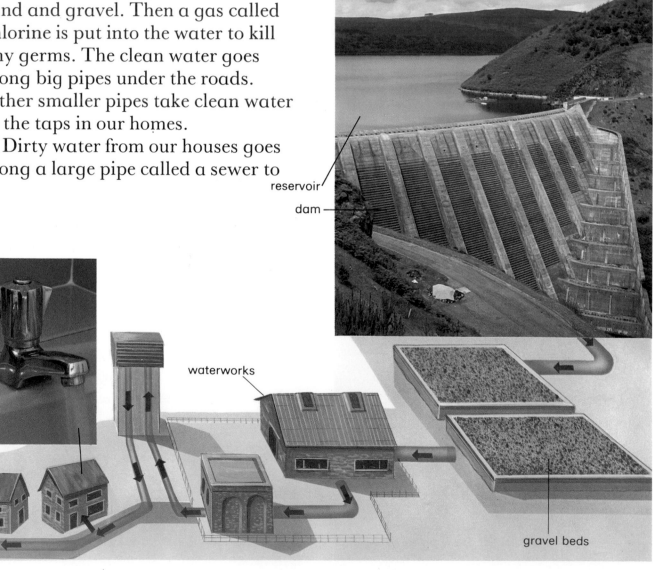

reservoir

dam

waterworks

gravel beds

Pollution

River pollution caused by a smelting works

Chemical crop spraying

Inset: Fish cannot survive in polluted water

Many towns and factories are built near rivers so that they can use the water. But some of these towns and factories do not clean the water before they put it back in the rivers. The water may even contain poisonous substances. This dirtying of water (and of the air and soil) is called pollution.

Another kind of pollution comes from chemicals put on fields to make the crops grow better. These chemicals, or fertilizers, are often washed from the fields by rain into streams and rivers. Chemicals put on fields to kill insect pests and weeds also get into streams and rivers. Thoughtless people sometimes dump rubbish in rivers.

Pollution makes rivers smell. It kills water plants and animals. It makes the water unfit for human use. Even the sea becomes polluted by the substances dumped into rivers. Rivers are precious treasures, and we ought to take great care of them.

Power from rivers

Hundreds of years ago people used fast-flowing rivers to turn their mills to grind corn. Some of these watermills can still be seen today. Watermills were also used to drive the machines which made wool and cotton cloth.

Nowadays electricity is sometimes made by using water to turn a big water-wheel. This big water-wheel is called a turbine. Water from a fast-flowing river on a hillside or mountain is led by pipes into a power station. There the water turns the turbines. The turbines turn the generators which make electricity. This kind of power station is called a hydro-electric power station. Hydro-electric power stations are built where there are mountains and fast rivers.

In some countries, the tides in an estuary are used to turn the turbines which turn the generators to make electricity. There is one of these tidal power stations in the estuary of the River Rance in France.

A surviving watermill

Hydro-electric power station in Strathclyde, Scotland

A tidal power station on the River Rance at St. Malo, France

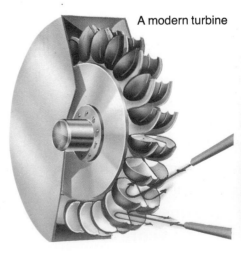

A modern turbine

18

Do you remember?

1 Roughly how much of the surface of the Earth is covered by oceans and seas?

2 What is ground water?

3 How do rivers change the landscape?

4 Give three reasons why the first villages might have been built near a river.

5 Why do many roads and railways follow river valleys?

6 What is a ford?

7 Name four ways in which we use water.

8 What is the invisible gas called which is formed when water is heated?

9 What are clouds made of?

10 What is meant by the water cycle?

11 What is an impermeable rock?

12 What is a permeable rock?

13 What is meant by the source of a river?

14 What are tributaries?

15 What is the area of land called which supplies a river with water?

16 What is a river like in its youthful stage?

17 What do we call the process by which rivers wear away rocks and carry the pieces towards the sea?

18 In which stage of a river would you find the most waterfalls?

19 How are waterfalls formed?

20 What is an estuary?

21 What are the wide S-shaped bends in a mature river called?

22 What is a delta and where is it formed?

23 How are caves formed in limestone hills or mountains?

24 What is a glacier?

25 What shape is the valley made by a glacier?

26 What is a reservoir?

27 How are any germs killed in our drinking water?

28 How is dirt removed from the water at a sewage works?

29 Name three ways in which a river may become polluted.

30 How is electricity made in a hydro-electric power station?

Things to do

1 Study your local river or stream

Choose a river or stream near your home or school and make a study of it. Only go there with the permission of a parent or teacher.

Make a sketch map of the river or stream. Mark on it any towns or villages. Where is the source of the river or stream? Is it a tributary of a bigger river? Where is the mouth of your river or stream? Find out from a map how long the river or stream is.

When you drop a twig into the water, does it move slowly or quickly? Can you hear the water moving?

Find out, by asking anglers, what fish are found in your river or stream. What do local people use the river or stream for? What other uses does the river or stream have?

2 The rate of flow of a stream

Study the rate of flow of a stream. Use a rubber ball or a stoppered plastic bottle partly filled with water to do this. See how long the ball or bottle takes to travel over a measured distance, say 5 metres.

Record the rate of flow in different places along the stream. At the same time, record how wide and how deep the stream is.

Does the stream flow faster where it is deep or shallow? Does the stream flow faster where it is wide or narrow?

Look at the materials which make up the bottom of the stream in the different places you study. Do these materials differ where the stream is flowing fast or slow?

3 Water to drink

Do you have a pet at home? Do you give it clean water each day? How much does it drink each day?

How much water and other liquids do you drink in a day? Keep a record of all the cups of milk, lemonade, squash, tea and other drinks you have in a day. How many litres do these add up to?

5 metres

4 Find out about evaporation

Find out about evaporation. Get a saucer and a small meat paste jar. Fill the jar to the top with water. Carefully empty this water into the saucer. Stand the saucer on a windowsill or shelf indoors. Fill the paste jar to the top again with water. Stand it by the side of the saucer of water. What happens to the water after a day or so? Which dries up first? Why? Where has the water gone?

5 Water in the air

Find out about water in the air. Take the label off an empty cocoa or coffee tin, or a can that has had vegetables or fruit in it. Carefully wash out the tin until it is clean. Fill the tin with ice cubes. Leave the tin in the room for a little while. Then look at the outside of it. Feel it. What has happened to the outside of the tin? Why?

Try this on a dry day and again on a wet day. Does the weather make any difference to what happens?

6 Drops of water

Carefully hold a cold spoon near the spout of a kettle of boiling water. See how the little drops of water collect together to form larger drops which fall like rain. Something similar to this happens in a cloud when raindrops form.

7 Water breaks down rocks

You can see how running water in streams and rivers breaks down rocks. Break some chalk into small pieces (blackboard chalk will do). Chalk is a soft rock and will break more easily. It would take a long time for this experiment to work if you used harder rocks.

Half fill a bottle with water. Put some of the pieces of chalk in the water. Put the stopper on the bottle and shake the bottle hard. Be careful not to drop the bottle. Shake the bottle for as long as you can.

Then look at the pieces of chalk. How do they differ from pieces that have not been shaken with water? What can you see at the bottom of the bottle?

You could also try this experiment with small pieces of brick. Do you get the same results?

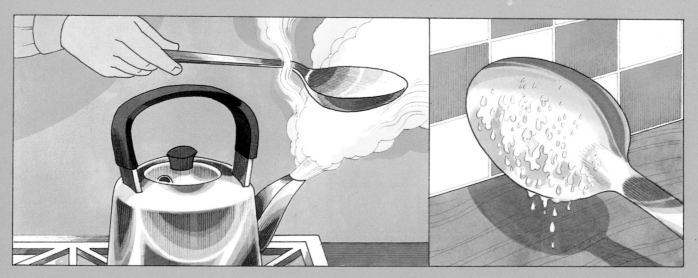

8 Layers of rock Find a jar with a wide mouth. Stand the jar in a bowl to protect the table.

Collect samples of mud from several different places. Mix several spoonfuls of one of the samples of mud with a cupful of water in an old jug. Then pour all the muddy water into the jar.

Wait until the water in the jar has cleared. This may take several hours, or even a day or so. Then pour in a different sample of mud and water into the jar. Later still, when the water has cleared do this again.

You may have to tip some of the water out of the jar to stop it from overflowing. But try not to stir up the mud at the bottom of the jar.

Can you see why the mud samples form separate layers in the jar? Mud is made up of tiny rock particles. Which rock particles sink faster – the larger or the smaller ones? Which of the layers was the first one you put in the jar? Which layer was put in last?

When a river carries pieces of rock, which pieces do you think would settle out first? Can you think why the mud layers left by a river should help plants grow?

9 Water dissolves substances from rocks Water dissolves some of the substances, called mineral salts, in rocks as it flows over them. This helps to break the rocks down. Plants take up some of these mineral salts through their roots and use them as food.

You can see these mineral salts if you half fill a clean jar with water from a river, stream, lake or pond.

Take a circular filter paper, or cut a circle from blotting paper. Fold the paper as shown in the picture.

Moisten the inside of a funnel with water and place the cone of paper inside it. Stand the funnel over another clean jar and slowly and carefully pour your sample of water into the paper. The paper sieves out, or filters, the small pieces of material floating in the water, so that the water now looks perfectly clean.

Put some of this clear water in a clean white saucer. Leave the saucer of water near a radiator or on a sunny windowsill. The water will evaporate and you will see the mineral salts left around the saucer. What colour are the mineral salts? Compare different samples of water. Which contains the most mineral salts?

10 Dissolving chalk or limestone Rainwater will slowly dissolve chalk or limestone. This is because, as it falls, rainwater dissolves carbon dioxide gas from the air. The rainwater becomes a very weak acid which will dissolve the limestone or chalk.

Vinegar is also a weak acid. You can see how chalk or limestone is dissolved if you

12 Pictures of boats Collect pictures of the different kinds of ships and boats which sail on rivers. Stick your pictures in a book or make a wall chart of them. Write a sentence or two about each one.

put a small piece of one of these rocks in a saucer. Do not use blackboard chalk, this is a different substance from the chalk dug out of the ground. Pour a little vinegar on the chalk or limestone. Watch what happens. What do you see? What do you hear?

After an hour or two take the piece of chalk or limestone out of the vinegar. Does it feel different from pieces of the chalk or limestone which have not been put in vinegar?

11 Find out more about water pressure Take a tall plastic bottle. With a large nail make holes in it like those in the picture.

Stand the bottle in the sink and plug the holes with sticky tape. Fill the bottle with water. When the sticky tape is removed, water will flow out of the holes. From which hole does the strongest jet of water flow? Write a sentence to explain what happens. Use these words in the sentence: 'depth', 'pressure', 'increases'.

Can you see now why dams are thicker at the bottom than at the top?

own about rivers. Ask some friends to help you to make some music to go with your poem. Write your music down if you can.

15 Cleaning dirty water

Shake some soil in a jar with water. What colour is the water? Leave the jar to stand for two days. What happens to the water? What happens to the soil?

Put a layer of cotton wool in the bottom of a flower pot. On top of this put a layer of clean gravel about 3 or 4 centimetres thick. Cover the gravel with a layer of clean sand about 3 or 4 centimetres thick. Lay a piece of paper on top of the sand.

Stand the flower pot on top of a clean jar so that the drainage holes of the flower pot are over the jar.

Shake some soil up in a jar of water. Slowly and carefully pour the muddy water on to the piece of paper in the flower pot.

What is the water like which comes out of the flower pot into the jar at the bottom? Is it still muddy? Is it fit to drink?

The flower pot acts as a filter. It filters the soil out of the water. Is it possible to use your flower pot filter to get the salt out of salty water?

16 Algae and water pollution

Water often looks green because it contains thousands of tiny plants called algae. Collect a little of this green water from a pond, ditch, or farm puddle. Sometimes algae make the water in flower vases go green.

Divide your green water equally between two clean jam-jars. Stand the two jars next to each other on a sunny windowsill. Add two or three drops of washing-up liquid to one jar. Add a little plant fertilizer to the other (ask a grown-up for permission to do this). Watch both jars. What happens to the algae in each?

How would washing-up liquid or fertilizer get into a river?

13 Make a water wheel

Cut the metal foil top from a yoghurt pot, or cream carton. Make a small neat hole at the centre. Cut 8 slits at equal distances apart around the edge. Twist the eight pieces to make paddles. Push a knitting needle through the hole in the middle of the wheel.

Hold the water wheel under a running tap. Does the wheel go round? This is how a turbine at a hydro-electric power station is also turned (see page 18).

14 Poems about rivers

Find some poems about rivers. Copy them into your notebook. Try writing a little poem of your

Things to find out

1   During a heavy storm there may be 1 centimetre of rainfall. This means the water would fill a straight sided tin or jar to a depth of 1 centimetre.

Find out how many litres of water would fall on 1 square metre of land during 1 centimetre of rainfall. You can do this by experimenting with small containers and marking out a metre on the ground, or by simple calculation. How much does this water weigh?

Can you find out roughly how much water would fall on your playground during a 1 centimetre rainfall?

2   Write down some ways in which rivers can (a) help people, and (b) hinder people.

3   How quickly can water soak through sand? How quickly can it soak through pebbles? How quickly can it soak through clay? Test them to find out. What difference might this make to puddles on the ground?

4   Look at an atlas. Find some large cities. Are these cities built by rivers? Make a table showing the names of the cities and the names of the rivers by which they are built.

5   Make a list of towns, cities and villages which begin or end with 'ford' or 'bridge'. Two examples are Oxford and Cambridge. How many more can you find? What rivers are near these places?

6   What are the advantages of making electricity in hydro-electric power stations compared with the other methods? Why are there not more hydro-electric power stations?

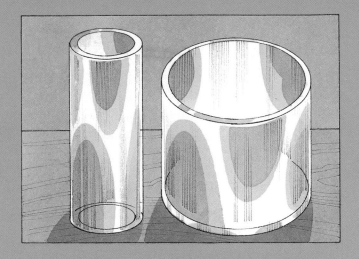

7   Look at the two jars in the picture. What is the difference between them? Suppose everything else is the same. If you stood the two jars out in the rain, in which jar would the rainwater be deeper? Why? Can you find two jars like this to test your ideas?

8   Some rivers (and many canals) have gates across them called locks. Find out what these locks are used for. When are they opened, and when are they closed?

9   Look at an atlas. Find out which rivers have large deltas. Draw some of these deltas to show the different shapes they make.

10   The picture shows two groups of pebbles. Which pebbles have been moved farther by water? How do you know?

River plants

Few plants can grow in the youthful parts of a river. But clinging to the rocks there may be some simple plants called algae.

In the mature regions of the river more plants can grow. They are rooted in the mud and sand at the bottom of the river. Where the river is flowing quite fast, the leaves of the plants are long and narrow. They bend and sway with the current. If the leaves were wide the plants would be swept away.

In the slow-flowing parts of a river, plants can grow in the mud at the bottom. The large leaves and flowers of water lilies can float on the surface of the water. Plants can also grow at the sides of slow-flowing rivers.

In the estuaries and deltas of rivers, mud is always being deposited. The water also contains salt from the seawater brought in by the tides. The plants which grow in estuaries have to be able to withstand

Algae growing on rocks

Narrow leaved water weeds

Water lily in bloom

the salt and mud. The mud is trapped among the leaves and stems of these plants. Gradually these plants help to build up the banks of sand and mud so that they become dry land.

Yellow flag iris

Few plants can grow in the salt water of estuaries

26

River animals

Rivers plants are food for some river animals. So are the tree leaves and other pieces of plants which fall into rivers. Water shrimps, water snails and other small animals feed on the pieces of plants. So do some fish such as carp. Other fish are hunters or predators. The plant-eaters are food for some of these predatory fish. Pike, perch and chub are predatory fish. They feed on the plant-eaters as well as on other fish.

By far the greatest variety of fish live in tropical rivers. The Amazon River contains about 2000 kinds of fish. The fiercest of these are piranhas. Each piranha is no more than 60 centimetres long. Usually they feed on smaller fish. But a shoal of piranhas can eat a whole cow in a few minutes.

Some land birds and animals come to rivers to catch fish. Kingfishers, herons and otters often fish in rivers. A few animals come to rivers to breed. Frogs, toads, dragonflies and damselflies all lay their eggs in water. Some water birds build their nests on or by rivers. And many other land birds and animals gather at rivers to drink.

A damselfly on a reed

The malachite kingfisher

The brown trout

Otters are excellent swimmers

Trout, salmon and eels

Most river fish spend all their lives in rivers. Rainbow trout and brown trout spend all their lives in the area where they were born. But not all river fish stay in one place. Most salmon hatch from eggs laid in rivers. The young salmon swim down to the sea. There they grow into adult fish. They stay in the sea for a year or two, feeding on small sea creatures. Then the salmon start on the long journey back to the river where they were born.

It is believed that every river has its own particular smell. When the salmon get near the coast, they smell their way towards the place where they were born. When they reach their birthplace the salmon spawn. Soon afterwards they die.

Like salmon, eels also migrate. They spend most of their life in a river. But when the time comes for

Leaping salmon on the River Lledr, Wales

them to breed, eels swim down to the sea. European eels swim out to the Sargasso Sea, an area of floating seaweed in the Atlantic Ocean. That is where the young eels are born. Later the young eels swim inland up rivers. There they live for several years before they too go back to the sea to breed.

Young eels or elvers migrating inland

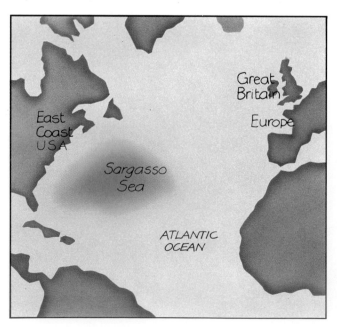

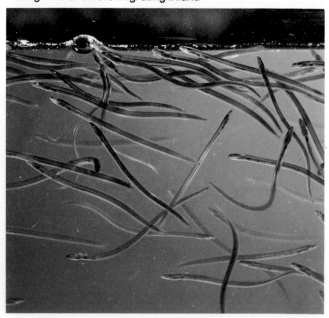

28

The River Rhine

Two hundred years ago roads were poor and railways had not been invented. Rivers were often the best way to get about. Boats and barges were also the only easy way to carry heavy cargoes.

Some rivers are still important as highways. One of these is the River Rhine in Europe. The Rhine is the busiest river in the world. It flows from the Swiss Alps to the North Sea. Where it enters the North Sea, in the Netherlands, the Rhine forms a huge delta.

On the Rhine, barges carry iron ore, steel, coal, petrol and other heavy cargoes. A new port has been built where the Rhine enters the sea near Rotterdam. It is called Europort. From Europort, cargoes are sent to and received from all parts of the world.

Rhine barge

One of the Rhine's many floating hotels

Many holiday-makers also travel along the Rhine in special floating hotels. They go to relax and enjoy the beautiful scenery along the Rhine valley.

The new port of Europort

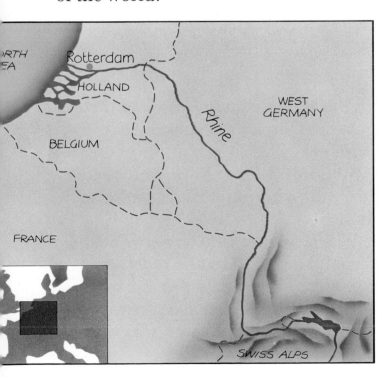

The Rhine delta

The Rhine Delta

As we saw on page 13, the mud carried by a river may be dropped near its mouth. This mud may form a new piece of land called a delta. But deltas are not always solid. Sometimes lakes develop within them. This happened with the delta at the mouth of the Rhine.

The Dutch people have changed these delta lakes. The lakes have been cut off from the sea with walls of brick and stone called dykes. Pumps lift the water from the land. In the past the Dutch used windmills to do this work. The pumps lift the water into canals. More pumps and canals carry the water into rivers and away to the sea.

The new land which was formed by the mud dropped by the river is called a polder. The polders become very fertile farmland. The Dutch grow wheat, barley, sugarbeet, flax and other crops on the polders.

The River Thames

By the late 1950s, Britain's most important river, the River Thames, was almost dead. The water of London's river was so polluted that it was black in colour. It also smelled strongly.

Now the River Thames is changing. The water is getting cleaner. One reason is that ships are getting bigger. Many of London's old docks have closed down. A new port has been built near the mouth of the river where it is wider and deeper. New sewage works have also been built. Factories have to pass their wastes to the sewage works instead of putting them straight in the river. Now the water birds, fish and other wild life are returning to the River Thames.

But there is another danger on the Thames. This is the danger of tidal surges. These occur when a high tide is blown inland by strong winds. This causes the water level to rise rapidly.

Polluted banks of the Thames at Wandsworth, London
Swans at Rotherhithe

London was always in danger of being flooded. Now a large moveable barrier has been built across the Thames. Usually this barrier is open so that ships can pass through. But when there is a risk of flooding from a tidal surge, the barrier is closed.

London's dilapidated docklands   The Thames Barrier

The River Amazon

The River Amazon is, with the River Nile, one of the two largest rivers in the world. The Amazon flows nearly 6500 kilometres across South America. It begins as hundreds of tiny streams in the Andes of Peru in the west. It flows to the Atlantic Ocean in the east. Hundreds more tributaries flow into the main river. These tributaries and the land between them make up the Amazon drainage basin.

Much of the Amazon basin is taken up with hot, steamy forest. This whole forest is more than ten times the size of England. Rain falls on more than 200 days every year. As a result the Amazon carries more water than any other river.

At one time few people went to the Amazon basin. But now oil and minerals have been discovered. In addition the forests contain valuable timber trees including teak, mahogany and rosewood. Rubber trees, Brazil nuts, and jute to make sacking and the backing of carpets, are also grown there. Large roads have been made through the forest. And huge areas have been cut down to make room for villages, towns, and fields where crops can be grown and cattle can graze. These changes mean that more mud and pollution now enter the Amazon, and soil erosion is widespread.

Forest clearance at Carajas, Brazil

The Amazon flowing on its way to the Atlantic

River dwellings at Manaus, in central Brazil

The Colorado River

The Colorado River rises in the Rocky Mountains of North America. Its source is the water from the melting winter snows. It is mostly this snow which keeps the river flowing for 2320 kilometres across desert country.

Halfway down the Colorado River its swift waters run through the famous Grand Canyon. This steep-sided valley is 2 kilometres deep in places. The Grand Canyon was carved over thousands of years by the rocks, boulders, pebbles and sand grains carried by the powerful current. Canyons are formed where the rock is hard and where the sides of the valley do not wear down easily. The Grand Canyon has been made

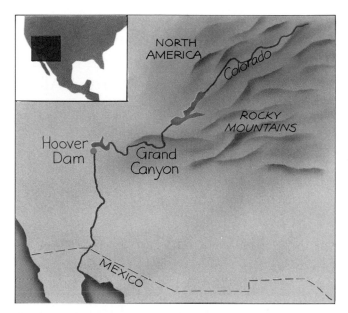

deeper because, long ago, the land over which the river flows was pushed up. This made the river flow faster because the land was steeper. And the faster river cut its valley deeper.

The Colorado River used to flood from time to time. Other years it dried up completely. Several dams have now been built across it. The dams even out the water flow all the year round. They also make hydro-electricity.

The Grand Canyon

The Boulder Dam

The River Nile

The River Nile is the longest river in Africa. Its two main tributaries, the Blue Nile and the White Nile, rise in areas where there is heavy rain. After the Blue Nile and White Nile join, however, they flow across one of the driest places in the world. Much of the land is barren desert.

At one time the Nile used to flood its banks each autumn. The water and mud left behind by the floods allowed the desert to be farmed along the edges of the Nile. The ancient Egyptians also developed irrigation. They dug canals to carry water from the Nile to their fields. Water was tipped on to the fields from a shaduf or an Archimedes' screw. But as the population of Egypt grew there was not always enough water for everyone.

By building a number of dams the Egyptians have controlled the flow of the Nile. The biggest dam is at Aswan. It holds the water back in a huge reservoir called Lake Nasser. Small canals carry some of the water away to fields and villages. Water rushing over the dam also provides the energy to make electricity. Unfortunately a lot of water in Lake Nasser evaporates in the hot sun. And a lot of the mud which used to be spread on the fields when the river flooded now clogs up the reservoir.

A village on the Nile in Egypt

An Archimedes' screw raising water for irrigation

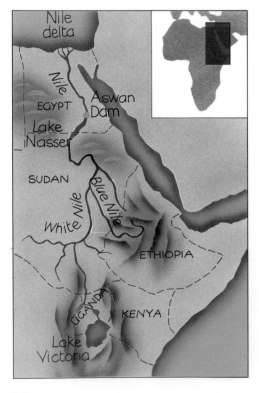

34

The Yangtse River

A junk at Shanghai

Rice cultivation near Canton

The Yangtse River in Shanghai

The Yangtse is the largest river in Asia. It runs for 6288 kilometres from the mountains of Tibet in the west. It has about 700 tributaries. The Yangtse enters the Yellow Sea near the port of Shanghai.

Almost half of the crops eaten by the Chinese people are grown on the banks of the Yangtse. Rice, barley, maize, wheat and beans as well as cotton and hemp all grow on the rich farmland by this huge river.

The Yangtse is also one of the busiest rivers in the world. It is China's most important highway.

Large ships can travel up the river to reach Chungking, 2400 kilometres from the sea. Many smaller boats such as junks and sampans also carry cargoes and people along the Yangtse and its tributaries. A lot of people live on these boats all their lives, and they hardly ever set foot on land.

The Yangtse often floods after the heavy monsoon rains. There have been more than 1000 bad floods in 2000 years. Now the Chinese are building dams across the Yangtse to control its flow. These dams will also help to make hydro-electric power.

The Murray River

With its tributaries, including the Darling and Murrumbidgee, the Murray is the largest river system in Australia. The tributaries of the Murray arise in the Eastern Highlands of Australia where the rainfall is heavy. But the rivers flow westwards over the dry interior of Australia. The rivers flow very slowly across these flat, dry areas. Much of the water evaporates in the hot sunshine. In very dry summers the rivers almost stop flowing. The soil along the lower Murray River valley is dry but fertile.

There are many rivers flowing down the eastern side of the mountains. To improve the water supply to the interior of Australia, one of these rivers, the Snowy River, has been dammed. Much of its water now flows through tunnels to the Murray and Murrumbidgee Rivers. Hydro-electric power stations have also been built near some of the dams. Because of the water from the dams, sheep and cattle can be kept on what was once desert. Grapes, oranges, grapefruit and many other crops can be grown.

Orange groves at Mildura

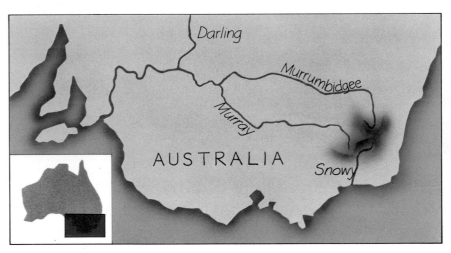
The Murray River

Some famous waterfalls

The spectacular Angel Falls in Venezuela

The Victoria Falls

There are thousands of small waterfalls in the world. The highest waterfalls on Earth are the Angel Falls in South America. They are deep in the jungle. No one knew the falls were there until 1935 when an American pilot, Jimmy Angel, first saw them from his aeroplane. The water drops 979 metres.

The most famous waterfalls are the Niagara Falls. They lie on the border between Canada and the United States of America. There are in fact two falls. The Horsehoe Falls are so named because of their shape. The other part is called the American Falls. Each year the Niagara Falls are worn back upstream about 1 metre by the rushing water and the pieces of rock it carries. In winter time it is so cold that the Niagara Falls freeze. Then huge icicles hang over the edge of the falls. Waterfalls make it impossible for boats to pass. But the Niagara Falls have been by-passed. A canal has been cut around the waterfalls. And a series of locks, like steps, carry ships up and down past the Falls.

The Victoria Falls are in Africa on the borders of Zambia and Zimbabwe. There the Zambesi River falls over a cliff 107 metres high. The spray thrown up by the falling water looks like smoke. It sounds like thunder.

Rivers for sport and leisure

Windsurfing in the Lake District

Boating on the Thames at Richmond, London

Rivers are places for leisure or sports activities. Many people like to walk or picnic by rivers. Rivers in the country, or which run through city parks, can be peaceful and quiet.

One of the oldest water sports is swimming. It is safe to swim in some rivers. In others it is dangerous because of pollution or strong currents. Rowing and sailing are two more river sports or pastimes. So also is the sport of water-skiing.

The most popular river sport of all

Fishing on the River Shannon in Ireland

is angling or fishing. There are two main kinds of river angling. Game angling is for trout and salmon. Game anglers often use a hook disguised to look like one of the insects the trout or salmon feed on. Game anglers often keep the fish they catch to eat. Coarse angling is for the slower fish such as roach, tench, chub, bream or perch. Most coarse anglers put the fish they catch back in the river again. The sport is in catching and landing the fish.

Do you remember?

1 What are the simple plants called which grow in the youthful parts of a river?

2 Why do the plants in the faster-flowing parts of a river have long and narrow leaves?

3 How do the plants in an estuary or delta help to make dry land?

4 What shape are the fish in fast-flowing rivers?

5 Which kinds of rivers contain the greatest number of fish?

6 How do adult salmon find their way back to the rivers where they were born?

7 Where do European eels breed?

8 Where is the source of the River Rhine?

9 What is the name of the new port which has been built near the mouth of the River Rhine?

10 How do many holiday-makers travel along the River Rhine?

11 What have the Dutch people done to the delta lakes at the mouth of the River Rhine?

12 What is the new land called which was formed from mud dropped by the River Rhine?

13 What has been done to make the River Thames cleaner?

14 What causes a tidal surge?

15 What has been done on the River Thames to prevent tidal surges leading to floods?

16 Which are the two longest rivers in the world?

17 Into which ocean does the River Amazon flow?

18 What is the Amazon's drainage basin like?

19 Where does most of the water in the Colorado River come from?

20 What happened to make the Grand Canyon even deeper than it would otherwise have been?

21 What are the names of the two main tributaries of the River Nile?

22 How did the Egyptians first irrigate the fields using water from the River Nile?

23 What have the Egyptians done to control the flow of the River Nile?

24 What are two ways in which the Yangtse River is important to the Chinese?

25 Name two kinds of boat which travel up the Yangtse River.

26 What has been done in Australia to make the Murray River contain more water?

27 Where is the highest waterfall in the world and what is it called?

28 What has been done so that ships can travel past the Niagara Falls in the United States?

29 Name four sports which people carry out on rivers.

Things to do

1 Studying freshwater life The best way to learn about life in running water is to visit a stream and study the animals that live there. Any stream will do if it is shallow enough to wade in.

The best time for studying freshwater life is in the summer and early autumn. The water is usually clear then and the animals are most active. In the spring the water is often too high and too muddy for easy observation. In the winter many of the animals burrow in the mud at the bottom and hide until the warmer weather returns. Even so, a good many creatures remain active throughout the year.

Many animals can be caught with no equipment at all. Insects that cling to stones or plant stems can simply be picked off by hand. Better still, is to gently pick them up by brushing them, with a small paint brush, into a plastic spoon. To catch some of the larger and more active animals you will need a net (see number 2).

Since much of the animal life in streams is small and camouflaged, it is most easily looked at against a white background. A white enamel pie dish or a white plate or soup bowl is ideal for this. A hand lens or magnifying glass is also very useful to help you to see the animals in more detail.

It is important that any stones you turn over when looking for animals are put back exactly where you found them. Do not take away more than one or two creatures of each kind, and return them to the stream when you have finished looking at them.

Keep a record of when and where you found the different kinds of animals and plants. Sketches and maps will make your records complete.

Ask your teacher if you can set up an aquarium so that you can keep some freshwater life for a week or two.

2   A dip net   To catch insects and other small animals as they swim through the water, use a dip net made from an ordinary kitchen gravy strainer. For best results, tape or wire the strainer to a handle about 1 metre long – an old broom stick makes a good handle.

You can make larger nets by sewing a sturdy wire hoop into the opening of a bag made of fine-meshed fabric. Fix this to a wooden handle.

Sweep the net back and forth in the water. Empty the contents from time to time into a white tray, together with a little water, so that you can look at them more closely.

3   An underwater viewer   Find a large tin to make an underwater viewer. Remove the top and bottom with a tin opener. Carefully hammer down any sharp pieces. Cover the top and bottom rims of the tin with insulating tape.

Cover one end of the tin with transparent plastic. Fix this tightly with a rubber band.

Put the plastic-covered end of the viewer just below the surface of the water. Look through the open end to see what is happening under water. For best results work on a bright, sunny day. But avoid standing where you will cast a shadow on the area of water you wish to study.

Use your viewer only in places where a grown-up says it is safe to do so.

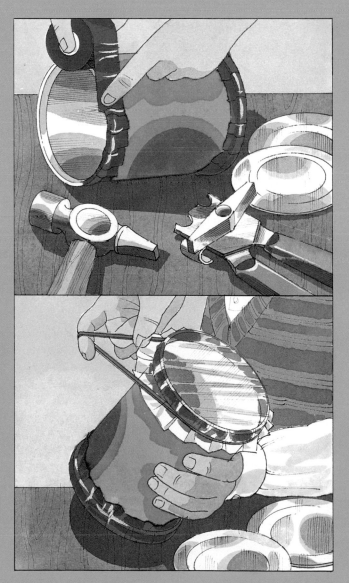

4 Study water snails Set up a large jar, plastic sandwich box or a small aquarium containing water from a river, stream or pond. Place a piece of waterweed in the container. Stand it on a sunny windowsill.

When the weed is growing well, put two water snails in the jar.

Watch the snails move and feed. How much do they eat each day? If the snails lay eggs, watch these hatch. The eggs are laid in a jelly-like mass. Look at them each day with a hand lens or magnifying glass. How long do they take to hatch?

5 Gnats and mosquitoes During the summer look on the surface of still water for gnat or mosquito larvae. They are easily reared to the adult form in jam-jars containing pond water, river water, or the stale water from a vase of flowers. Keep the jars out of doors.

Use a magnifying glass or hand lens to study the different stages in the life of a gnat or mosquito.

Why are mosquitoes feared in tropical parts of the world? What can be done to control the numbers of gnats and mosquitoes?

Mosquito larvae

6 Algae Algae can be found in most rivers, streams and ponds. They may look like a green scum on the water if the water is still. Other algae look like tufts of green cotton wool. Find a river, stream or pond near you and collect some algae.

If you or one of your friends has an aquarium, you may find algae growing on the sides.

Place a little piece of the algae under a microscope. What do the plants look like? Can you see cells? What do the cells look like? What colour are they? The green matter in the cells is called chlorophyll. Using chlorophyll, green plants can make their food.

7 An experiment on floating and sinking Put a milk bottle top in a bowl of water. Does it float? Now roll the bottle top tightly into a ball. You may need to use a hammer to roll the bottle top into a tight ball. Put the bottle top on the water. Does it float?

Make a plasticine boat that floats. Now roll the plasticine into a ball. Put it on the water. Does it float?

Can you understand now why ships made of steel can float?

8 Floating cans Put an empty cocoa or coffee tin in a bowl of water. Does it float? Use a marker pen to mark how far the water comes up the side of the can. Mark how far the water comes up the inside of the bowl.

Put a piece of clay or plasticine in the tin. How far does the water come up the side of the tin now? How far does the water come up the side of the bowl? What happens if you put still more clay or plasticine in the tin?

Do this experiment again, but this time keep a record of the weight of the empty tin and the weight of the clay or plasticine you put in it. What weight of clay or plasticine will the tin hold and still remain floating? What weight of clay or plasticine makes the tin sink?

Try this experiment again using the same tin and the same pieces of plasticine or clay. Put salt water in the bowl this time instead of tap water. What differences do you notice?

Does a ship float deeper in the water when it is carrying a heavy cargo? What happens when a ship sails from a river into the sea? Does it float deeper or less deep?

9   Water carries materials   After a heavy shower of rain, visit your local river or stream. Is the water cloudy or clear? If the water is cloudy, carefully collect a jar or bottle of it. Stand the jar or bottle on a windowsill. Watch the materials in the water settle. What kinds of materials are they? In what order do they settle?

10   Floods   Collect pictures and newspaper cutting about floods. Make a wallchart of your pictures and cuttings.

11   Compare river life with life in the sea   Collect pictures of some of the animals and plants that live in rivers and also of those which live in the sea. Make wallcharts with your pictures. Are there any plants or animals, apart from salmon and eels, which can live in both the sea and rivers?

12   A mudpie mountain   If you can obtain permission, make a mudpie mountain in the garden. Pat the mud down smooth. Push some stones into the mud and then let it dry.

Water your mountain with water from a watering can which is fitted with a spray. Where does the water wash away, or erode, your mountain? Are any valleys or gorges formed? Are there any waterfalls? Where does the mud which is eroded away finish up?

13   Oxygen in water   Animals living in water need a gas called oxygen to breathe. Some get this oxygen from the air at the surface. But water plants also give off oxygen when they make their food. Plants need sunlight to make food and to produce oxygen.

Try the experiment shown in the picture. Put some water weed in the jar of water. Stand it in the sun. Oxygen bubbles will soon appear and rise to the top of the jar.

14   Water and dissolved air
Take a clean jam-jar and put some cold water in it. Let the jar warm up by placing it near a radiator or on a sunny windowsill. Can you see tiny bubbles of air rising in the water? This air was dissolved in the water but comes out when you heat the water. Fishes use their gills to breathe the air which is dissolved in water.

15   A model of the Grand Canyon
Make a model of a part of the Grand Canyon. Use a piece of wire netting as a foundation. Crumple the wire netting into the shape you need (careful, the wire may be sharp!).

Cut a newspaper into strips about 2 centimetres wide. Mix a small bowlful of thin cold-water glue or wallpaper paste. Wet strips of the newspaper with the glue or paste. Cover the wire netting with the strips. See that all the wire netting is covered with several layers of newspaper.

Leave your model on one side. When the newspaper has dried out completely, paint your model. Do not forget to paint in the Colorado River.

Make models of other river scenes. Use some of the pictures in this or other books to give you ideas.

16 Bridges Look at the different kinds of bridges which are used to cross rivers. What materials are used to make these bridges? How do old bridges differ from more modern ones?

Collect pictures of river bridges. Make a wallchart or book of your pictures. Write a sentence or two about each one.

Make models of different kinds of bridges. Use waste materials to make them with. Carry out tests on your bridges to see which is the strongest.

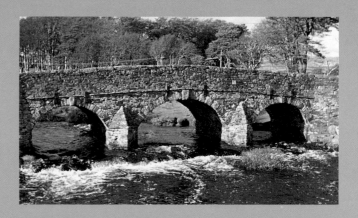

17 Songs about rivers Many song writers have written about rivers. 'Ol' Man River,' 'Old Father Thames,' and 'Shenandoah,' are just three songs about rivers. There are also songs about bridges. Listen to, sing or read songs about rivers and bridges. Can you write your own song about a river?

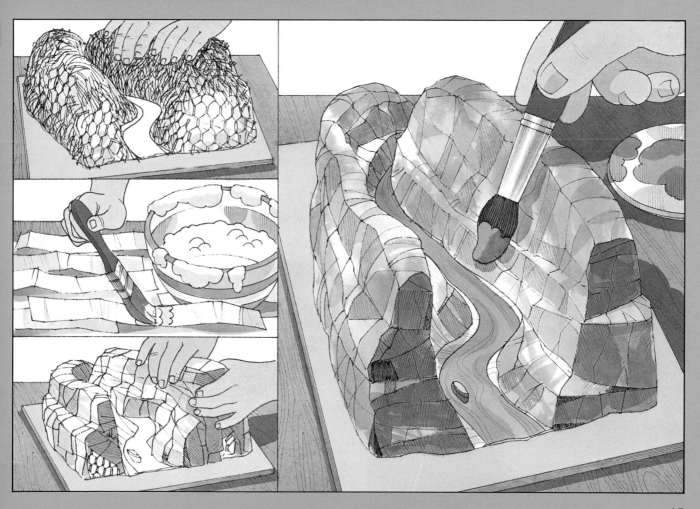

Things to find out

1 Find out more about the animals, such as otters, crocodiles, alligators and hippopotamuses, as well as the birds, which live on or by rivers.

2 Often in low-lying areas, rivers are straightened and made deeper. Why is this done even where ships do not use the river?

3 Here are some rivers not dealt with in this book: Severn, Danube, Mississippi, Ganges, Seine, Congo. Find out where they are and something interesting about each one of them.

4 In some parts of the world, rivers are used to carry logs to the timberyards. Find out where this is done and how the logs are actually carried by the river to the timberyards.

Log transportation in Vancouver, Canada

5 Look at an atlas. Find out which countries the River Rhine flows through. Between which countries does the Rhine form the boundary?

6 At many ports, cargoes are unloaded from ships on to barges. The barges then take the cargoes up rivers or canals. Why are barges used instead of ships to carry these cargoes? Why are the barges used instead of lorries or trains?

7 Rice is one of the main food crops in many countries. Find out where rice is grown and how it is looked after. How does the mud carried by rivers help rice to grow?

8 Many ships and barges now carry their cargoes in containers. Find out why it is better to carry cargoes in containers, rather than to carry them loose.

9 Why are rivers more likely to flood if forests in their drainage basins are cut down?

10 Pretend you are going to make a journey down the River Congo or River Amazon from its source to its mouth. Look at an atlas to see which places you might pass. What kind of country would you be crossing? Write a story describing some of the adventures you have.

Glossary

Here are the meanings of some words which you might have met for the first time in this book.

Algae: very simple plants without stems or leaves.

Canyon: a large deep river valley which has steep sides.

Dam: a large wall or bank built to hold back water and to raise its level. A large lake called a reservoir is often formed behind the dam.

Delta: an area of flat land at the mouth of a river made up of mud dumped there by the river. Many deltas are shaped like a triangle.

Drainage basin: the area of land which supplies a river with water.

Dredger: a special ship used to clear mud from a river or harbour.

Earth's crust: the Earth's outer layer of rock and soil on which we live.

Erosion: the wearing away of the land.

Estuary: the wide mouth of a river where fresh water meets sea water.

Evaporate: when water is heated it disappears into the air as water vapour. We say the water has evaporated.

Ford: a shallow place where a river can be crossed easily.

Glacier: a large river of ice which flows very slowly down a valley.

Ground water: the water in rocks, soil and other places below the surface of the ground.

Hanging valley: a valley which was made by a tributary of a glacier.

Hydro-electric power station: a power station which uses the force of running water to turn the generators which make electricity.

Impermeable rock: a rock which does not allow water to soak into it.

Irrigation: watering the land by artificial means so that crops will grow.

Larva: (*larvae*-plural): the stage in some insects' development between the egg and the adult.

Levee: a river bank made from material dumped by a river when it floods. Artificial levees keep the river in its channel.

Meander: a large S-shaped bend in a river.

Migrate: the moving from one place to another from time to time by animals or people.

Ox-bow lake: a lake made when a river changes course and cuts off a meander.

Permeable rock: a rock through which water can seep.

Plunge pool: the deep pool cut out by the swirling round of rocks and stones at the base of a waterfall.

Polder: a Dutch word for the new land made by draining the delta lakes at the mouth of a river.

Pollution: the dirtying of air, water or the soil.

Reservoir: a large artificial lake in which water for drinking, making electricity or watering fields is stored.

Sewage works: where dirty water is cleaned so that it can be put in rivers or sometimes into the sea.

Sewer: a large pipe which carries dirty water.

Source: the place where a river rises.

Spring: where underground water comes to the surface. Many streams and rivers start off as springs.

Stalactites and stalagmites: pieces of limestone like large icicles which are found in limestone caves. Stalactites hang down from the roof of a cave, stalagmites grow up from the floor of the cave.

Tidal surge: the sudden rise in water level in a river when a high tide is blown inland.

Tributary: a river or stream which flows into another larger river or stream.

Water cycle: the process by which water evaporates from the sea, lakes and other wet places and forms water vapour. This cools, falls as rain or snow and eventually goes back into lakes or the sea. And so the same water goes round and round.

Waterfall: a sudden fall of water over a step or ledge in the bed of a river.

Water vapour: the invisible gas which is formed when water is heated.

Index